HE KNEW MY NAME

What the Bible Teaches about the Sanctity of Life in the Womb

F. Wayne Mac Leod

Light To My Path Book Distribution

CONTENTS

PREFACE

The motivation for this study was a brief conversation I had with a brother in Christ about his concern with the practice of abortion in our day. This, however, is not a study about abortion. I am not qualified to do such a study. As I reflected on this matter, however, I felt the need to examine the teaching of Scripture about life in the womb and the plan of God even before conception.

In this study, we will examine the teachings of both the Old and New Testaments about the value of life in the womb. We will see how the hand of God not only forms the small child but also prepares this life for His purpose. It is my desire that we would see the fruit of the womb as God sees it and that our hearts would be encouraged to see the preciousness and value of life before birth.

May the Lord be pleased to use this study to bless and encourage you in your reflection on this important time of life.

F. Wayne Mac Leod

1 - KNOWN BEFORE CONCEPTION

God said, "No but Sarah your wife shall bear you a son, and you shall call his name Isaac. I will establish my covenant with him as an everlasting covenant for his offspring after him." (Genesis 17:19)

As we begin our study, let's go back to the book of Genesis and the promise of God to give Abraham a son. Abraham's wife Sarah was unable to conceive. This was a source of grief for them both. In Genesis 17, however, the Lord appeared to Abraham and told him that He would make of him a great nation and kings would be in his family line. Abraham laughed in disbelief at this word saying:

17 ...Shall a child be born to a man who is a hundred years old? Shall Sarah, who is ninety years old, bear a child? (Genesis 17:17)

God assured him, however, that his wife Sarah would indeed give him a son in her old age. In fact, the Lord promised Abraham that He would enter a special relationship with this child (Genesis 17:19). God told Abraham to call his son Isaac meaning "laughter"—a reference either to their disbelief when God told them they would have a child in their old age or to the joy and laughter that this child would bring them (particularly to Sarah who had been unable to have a child all her life).

Although Abraham had another son by the name of Ishmael, God told him that He had a special plan for Isaac:

> *20 As for Ishmael, I have heard you; behold, I have blessed him and will make him fruitful and multiply him greatly. He shall father twelve princes, and I will make him into a great nation. 21 But I will establish my covenant with Isaac, whom Sarah shall bear to you this time next year. (Genesis 17:20-21*

Isaac was very special to God. Notice in Genesis 17:21 how God calls him by name. He does this even before Isaac was conceived! It would not be for another year that this child would be born (Genesis 17:21).

Isaac is not the only child in Scripture to be described in this way. In Judges 13, we see how the people of God "did evil in the sight of the Lord, so the Lord gave them into the hand of the Philistines for forty years" (Judges 13:1). At that time an angel of the Lord appeared to another barren woman with a message:

3 ... Behold, you are barren and have not borne children, but you shall conceive and bear a son. 4 Therefore be careful and drink no wine or strong drink, and eat nothing unclean, 5 for behold, you shall conceive and bear a son. No razor shall come upon his head, for the child shall be a Nazirite to God from the womb, and he shall begin to save Israel from the hand of the Philistines. (Judges 13:3-5)

This child, yet to be conceived, would be a male child set apart for God from birth as a Nazirite. He would be an instrument of God to save Israel from the hand of the Philistines. A Nazirite was an individual set apart by means of a special vow to God. Numbers 6 describes the obligations of such a person as long as they were under this vow. They were not to consume strong drink, touch a dead body or cut their hair.

Notice in Judges 13:4 that God told the child's mother that she was not to drink wine or strong drink. The reason she was not to do so was because the child she was yet to conceive was set apart by the Lord for a special purpose. Though not yet conceived, God had already set Samson apart for a specific task.

In Luke 1, an angel appeared to a priest by the name of Zechariah and his wife Elizabeth. This godly couple had no children. One day, as Zechariah was ministering in the temple, this angel appeared before him. He had a message for Zechariah:

13 But the angel said to him, "Do not be afraid, Zechariah, for your prayer has been heard, and your wife Elizabeth will bear you a son, and you shall call his name John. 14 And you will have joy and gladness, and many will rejoice at his birth, 15 for he will be great before the Lord. And he must not drink wine or strong drink, and he will be filled with the Holy Spirit, even from his mother's womb, 16 And he will turn many of the children of Israel to the Lord their God, 17 and he will go before him in the power of Elijah, to turn the hearts of the fathers to the children, and the disobedient to the wisdom of the just, to make ready for the Lord a people prepared. (Luke 1:13-17)

Notice, again, that the angel calls the yet-to-be conceived child by name. He tells his father that John would be filled with the Holy Spirit from his birth. He would be an instrument to turn many to the Lord. He would prepare the hearts of the people of God for the coming of the Messiah. God knew John by name and had a purpose for his life even before he was conceived.

Speaking about the final judgement, the Lord Jesus reminded his listeners that the day would come when the sheep and the goats would be separated and judged according to their deeds. Listen particularly to what He said in Matthew 2:34-35:

34 Then the King will say to those on his right,

"Come, you who are blessed by my Father, inherit the kingdom prepared for you from the foundation of the world. 35 For I was hungry and you gave me food, I was thirsty and you gave me drink, I was a stranger and you welcomed me.

What is important for us to note here in Jesus' words is the phrase: "inherit the kingdom prepared for you from the foundation of the world." The kingdom, according to Jesus, was prepared for these sheep from the foundation of the world. This means that God was preparing a place for them even before they were conceived in the womb. Just as he knew Isaac, Samson and John the Baptist, so the Lord knew us before we were conceived. From the very beginning of time, He has been preparing a place in His kingdom for us. He knows our story from beginning to end. He knew that story from the foundation of the world, way before we were conceived or even imagined in the human mind.

God's delight in us did not begin the moment we were born. He delighted and knew us even before we were conceived in our mother's womb. The apostle Paul marveled at this when he wrote:

3 Blessed be the God and Father of our Lord Jesus Christ, who has blessed us in Christ with every spiritual blessing in the heavenly places, 4 even as he chose us in him before the foundation of the world, that we should be holy and blameless before him. In love 5 he predestined us for adoption as sons through

Jesus Christ, according to the purpose of his will 6 to the praise of his glorious grace, with which he has blessed us in the Beloved. (Ephesians 1:3-6)

Paul teaches us that the Lord God chose us "before the foundation of the world." There are many ways of looking at this phrase. In the context of this study, however, we need to see that God had a purpose and plan for my life that goes back to before I was conceived. From the foundation of the earth, God knew me. He knew all about my life and the purpose I would fulfill in life.

God is not limited to time as we are. The yet unconceived child is as important to His purpose as the mature adult. He knows children, yet to be conceived, as well as He knows each of us. He values the unconceived as much as those born into this world. He had a purpose for Isaac, Samson and John the Baptist who had not yet been conceived. There is a whole host of children, yet to be conceived who are known and loved by God who has a purpose for them in the work of His kingdom. How beautiful it is to know that God did not start loving us when we were conceived in the womb. His love and purpose for us goes back to the foundation of the world where no human thought even imagined us.

For Consideration:

What did God know about Isaac, Samson and John the Baptist before they were conceived? What was His purpose for their lives before they were conceived in the womb?

What does it mean to be known before the foundation of the world?

God is not limited to time as we are. He loves the unconceived child as much as the one who is conceived in the womb. What does this teach us about the value of life and the purpose of God?

For Prayer:

Thank the Lord that He knew you from before the world began.

Thank the Lord that He had a purpose for you and your life from the beginning of time.

Ask the Lord to help you to honour Him with your life by becoming all He intended you to be.

Take a moment to praise the Lord for His understanding that is far greater than ours and is not limited to time.

2 - CALLED BEFORE BIRTH

Listen to me, O coastlands, and give attention, you peoples from afar. The Lord called me from the womb, from the body of my mother he named my name. (Isaiah 49:1)

We have seen how the Lord knew us even before we were conceived and had a purpose for our lives. We move now to the point of conception and the physical body that is being formed in the womb of the mother. In the passage quoted above, Isaiah tells us two things about this time in the womb.

First, Isaiah tells us that the Lord calls His people from the womb. The call of God on our lives did not begin the moment we were born. It began well before this at the foundation of the earth and put into effect when we were conceived in the womb of our mothers. The yet undeveloped child is being formed for a purpose in the womb of the mother.

Second, we learn from Isaiah 49:1 that the Lord calls His children in the womb by name—"from the body of my mother he named my name." There is something very personal about this truth. In our day, there is a belief that a fetus in the womb is not a person until he or she is born. This is not what this passage tells us. The Lord calls this unfinished form by name. The eyes and ears of this baby are not yet fully functional. Legs and arms are not completely formed, but God still calls this child by name.

Speaking to the prophet Jeremiah the Lord said:

Before I formed you in the womb I knew you, and before you were born I consecrated you; I appointed you a prophet to the nations. (Jeremiah 1:5)

Take note of what God said to Jeremiah. He knew him before he was formed in the womb. Notice also when God called Jeremiah to be a prophet to the nations –"Before you were born I consecrated you." The word "consecrate" has the sense of being set apart and dedicated to a particular purpose. God set Jeremiah apart to be a prophet to the nations when he was still an unfinished form in his mother's womb.

What was true of Jeremiah is also seen in the life of the apostle Paul. Listen to his testimony in Galatians 1:15-17:

15 But when he who had set me apart before I was born, and who called me by his grace, 16 was pleased to reveal his Son to me, in order that I might preach him among the Gentiles, I did not immediately consult with anyone, 17 nor did I go up to Jerusalem to those who were apostles before me, but I went away into Arabia, and returned again to Damascus.

When we consider the life of the apostle Paul, we sometimes feel that he was called to serve the Lord when he was on his way to Damascus. Paul, however, tells us that while he met Jesus and came to understand the purpose of God on that day, he had actually been called by God well before that time. He tells us in Galatians 1:15 that God had set him apart before birth. There in the womb of his mother, the apostle Paul was being shaped to be a servant of the Almighty God. Admittedly, he did not understand that call for many years. He served faithfully as a devout Jew and did the best he could with his limited understanding of that call. Only when Jesus revealed Himself to Paul on the road to Damascus, however, did Paul fully understand the purpose of God from the womb of his mother.

Writing in Isaiah 49:5 the prophet says:

And now the Lord says, he who formed me from the womb to be his servant, to bring Jacob back to him; and that Israel might be gathered to him—for I am honored in the eyes of the Lord and my God has become my strength.

The Lord formed Isaiah from the womb to be His

servant. This work of shaping and training us to be servants of God does not begin when we are old enough to reason and think for ourselves. It begins in the womb. God is shaping our personality. He is forming us into the instruments He wants us to be in the belly of our mothers.

The Lord spoke to the mother of Samson and told her:

> *3 Behold you are barren and have not borne children, but you shall conceive and bear a son. 4 Therefore be careful and drink no wine or strong drink, and eat nothing unclean. 5 for behold you shall conceive and bear a son. No razor shall come upon his head, for the child shall be a Nazirite to God from the womb, and he shall begin to save Israel from the hand of the Philistines. (Judges 13:3-5)*

Notice what God told Samson's mother that day: "The child shall be a Nazirite to God from the womb." A Nazirite was a person set aside by means of a special vow to the Lord. As a Nazirite, he was never to shave his hair, drink strong drink or touch a dead body. God told his mother not to drink wine or strong drink while she was pregnant with him. She acted on his behalf during the time Samson was in her womb. Samson's vow was effective the moment he was conceived.

In Genesis 25, Rebekah, Isaac's wife, became pregnant and conceived twins. There were complications with this pregnancy and she went to the Lord to ask Him what was going on in her womb. The Lord responded:

... Two nations are in your womb, and two peoples from within you shall be divided; the one shall be stronger than the other, the older shall serve the younger. (Genesis 25:23)

The children in Rebekah's womb had a purpose in the mind of God. Two nations were forming in Rebekah's womb and her boys had been called from their mother's womb to be the fathers of these nations.

What do we understand from these passages of Scripture? Do they not show us that the Lord God has a purpose for the life of the child developing in the womb? God calls these children while they are still in the womb and sets them aside for a particular purpose. Even before my brain and consciousness have developed sufficiently to be aware of that call, God has been working in my life and setting me apart. He calls my unformed frame by name and knows me personally.

For Consideration:

Do we need a completely formed body to be loved by God? What do we learn in this chapter about the love of God for even the body being formed in the womb of the mother?

Isaiah tells us that God calls us by name from the womb of our mothers. What does this teach us about the value of the child yet to be born?

When were Paul and Jeremiah called by God? What does this teach us about the purpose of God for the unformed child in the womb?

While Paul was called from the womb, it would not be until much later in life that he fully understood that call. What is the difference between being called and understanding or walking in the call of God?

What is the call of God on your life?

For Prayer:

Thank the Lord that His love for us does not depend on what we look like or if we are in perfect physical form. Thank Him that He loved you even when you were unformed in your mother's womb.

Ask the Lord to reveal to you the call He has placed on your life from the time you were in your mother's womb.

Ask God to help you to be faithful to His call and to live out that purpose in your life.

3 - LIFE IN THE WOMB

The children struggled together within her, and she said, "If it is thus, why is this happening to me?" So she went to inquire of the Lord. (Genesis 25:22)

In Genesis 25, we have the story of the birth of Esau and Jacob. Rebekah, their mother, was barren. Her husband Isaac prayed for her and God answered his prayers. Rebekah conceived twins in her womb. In the course of the pregnancy, Rebekah noticed that something strange was taking place. Genesis 25:22 tells us that "the children struggled together within her." Rebekah could feel this struggle in her womb.

Notice in Genesis 25:22 that the Bible calls the unborn in her womb, "children." The Hebrew word used here is the same word used to speak of a son or grandson. From God's perspective, though their bodies were not yet completely formed, Esau and Jacob were children. They were human beings from the moment of conception.

Notice also from Genesis 25:22 that these two children

were "struggling together within her." The Hebrew word used for "struggle" is quite strong. It literally means to crack in pieces, to break, to bruise, to crush, to oppress or to discourage. It is used, for example, in Deuteronomy 28:33-34:

> *33 A nation that you have not known shall eat up the fruit of your ground and of all your labors, and you shall be only oppressed and crushed continually, 34 so that you are driven mad by the sights that your eyes see.*

Notice in these verses that the people of God would be "crushed" to the point that they would be driven mad in their pain. The word translated "crushed" is the same word used to describe what the children in Rebekah's womb were doing to each other.

The same word is used in 2 Chronicles 16:10 to speak of Asa who "inflicted cruelties" on some of the people of the land. Judges 9:53 uses it to describe what happened to Abimelech when a woman dropped a millstone on his head.

When Genesis 25:22 tells us that the children struggled in the womb of their mother, we understand that there was a serious conflict taking place in Rebekah's womb. Rebekah became so concerned about this conflict that she brought the matter to the Lord. Listen to what the Lord told her in Genesis 22:23:

> *And the Lord said to her, "Two nations are in your*

womb, and two peoples from within you shall be divided; the one shall be stronger than the other, the older shall serve the younger."

The reason for this conflict in Rebekah's womb was that these two children were the fathers of two enemy nations. Notice particularly in Genesis 22:23 that these two nations would be divided from within their mother's womb. The conflict between these two nations began in as the two boys struggled with each other before their birth.

When the time for Rebekah to give birth arrived, Esau was born first. When Jacob was born, it was noted that he was grasping his brother's heal—a sign of hostility toward his brother. As these boys grew older, bitterness between them would grow. Jacob would steal Esau's birthright and blessing. Esau would swear to kill Jacob. The Edomites—descendants of Esau hated the Israelites and even generations later this hostility was still evident between the two nations.

Where did this hostility start? From Genesis 25 we understand that it started in Rebekah's womb. These two young boys were not fully conscious of what was taking place but their fighting and bitterness started before they were born. Something was happening in Rebekah that would impact generations of people. There was a spiritual battle taking place right there in her womb and these children were in the centre of that battle.

There is another example in Scripture we need to

consider in this regard. In Luke 1, we have the announcement of the birth of John the Baptist. Listen to what the angel told his father Zechariah:

15 for he will be great before the Lord. And he must not drink wine or strong drink, and he will be filled with the Holy Spirit, even from his mother's womb.

Notice when John the Baptist was filled with the Holy Spirit—"even from his mother's womb." The Holy Spirit of God was pleased to dwell in this unformed child and fill him with power even before he was born. Evidence of this filling is found in Luke 1:41:

41 And when Elizabeth heard the greetings of Mary, the baby leaped in her womb, And Elizabeth was filled with the Holy Spirit, 42 and she exclaimed with a loud cry, "Blessed are you among women and blessed is the fruit of your womb! 43 And why is this granted to me that the mother of my Lord should come to me? 44 For behold, when the sound of your greeting came to my ears, the baby in my womb leaped for joy.

On this particular occasion, Mary, who was pregnant with our Lord, came to see Elizabeth (the mother of John the Baptist). When Elizabeth heard the sound of Mary's greeting, John "leaped for joy" in her womb. The Spirit of God filled John in the womb. In response, Elizabeth prophesied, speaking a word of encouragement from the Lord to Mary. Even as there was a spiritual battle taking place in Jacob and Esau, so there was a work of God's Spirit in the life of John before he was born.

As we reflect on these two passages of Scripture we see that significant things happen in the womb of the mother. God is pleased to use the unfinished form of the child He is shaping. He does not wait until they are born to begin His work in and through them.

Consider this for a moment. The hand of God, who created the universe and sustains it, reaches down to the tiny seed in the womb of its mother and touches it in a special way. He fills that seed and begins to work out His purposes. There is something very holy about this. God's delight in me did not begin when I was born. It began farther back than this. He delighted in me from the womb. He began to work out His purposes in me from the womb of my mother.

For Consideration:

When did conflict between Esau and Jacob begin? What impact did this conflict have on generations to follow?

When was John the Baptist filled with the Holy Spirit? What evidence is there in Scripture of this filling from the womb?

What encouragement do you find from the fact that

God is willing to use the unfinished form of a child in the womb?

When does God begin His work in your life?

What do the passages we have examined here teach us about the value of life in the womb?

If God can use the unfinished form of a child in the womb how much does He need our strength and wisdom?

For Prayer:

Thank the Lord that He loved you before you were born and even when you were still in your mother's womb He knew you and was shaping you for the purpose He had in store for your life.

Take a moment to consider the value of life in the womb. Ask the Lord to help you to value this life as He does.

Ask the Lord to forgive you for believing that the Lord uses you because of your human strength and experience. Thank Him that He can use us even in our weakness and frailty.

4 - THE WORK OF GOD IN THE WOMB

For you formed my inward parts; you knitted me together in my mother's womb. O praise you, for I am fearfully and wonderfully made. (Psalm 139:13-14)

In the course of this study we have seen how God knew us before we were conceived and called us while we were yet in the womb. In the last chapter we examined how God can use and fill the life of the unborn child. Let's consider now three further works of God in the life of the unborn.

The Creative Work Of God In The Womb

The writers of Scripture marveled at the creative work of God in the mother's womb. I was present with my wife when all of our children were born. What an incredible thing it is to experience the birth of a child. There before us was a living and breathing child. Life was brought into this world. What we need to realize, however, is that the Lord God has been working in the life of this child well before his or her birth. The psalmist speaks of this in Psalm 139:13-14 when he says:

For you formed my inward parts; you knitted me together in my mother's womb. O praise you, for I am fearfully and wonderfully made.

The psalmist describes what was happening in the womb as God knitting a life together. He joins each individual part connecting one with the other until that life is complete and whole. The psalmist describes this work of God as fearful and wonderful. In other words, it is a work that inspires awe, reverence and praise.

Listen to what the prophet Isaiah told his people in Isaiah 44:2:

1 But now hear, O Jacob my servant, Israel whom I have chosen! 2 Thus says the Lord who made you, who formed you from the womb and will help you.

The word translated by the English word "formed" is used to describe the work of a potter who squeezes the clay on the wheel into the shape he wants. There is a very personal dimension to this image. God shapes each life personally in the womb. Each child is given his or her uniqueness by the heavenly Creator.

Isaiah repeats the same thought when he says:

24 Thus says the Lord, your Redeemer, who formed you from the womb: "I am the Lord who made all things, who alone stretched out the heavens, who spread out the earth by myself. (Isaiah 44:24)

Every child born into this world is a product of the creative genius of God who works to shape the child in the womb of the mother. The fact that each of us is different in looks and personality is an indication of the personal nature of this creative work of a God who shapes each one personally. That unborn child is a unique work of God in progress. God has taken a personal interest in each one and shapes them into the person He wants them to be. This process begins in the womb and is still one of life's greatest miracles.

The Protection Of God In The Womb

Not only does Scripture teach that God forms the unborn child but He also protects this child in the womb. The psalmist understood this when he wrote:

Upon you I have leaned from before my birth; you are he who took me from my mother's womb. My praise is continually of you. (Psalm 71:6)

Notice that the psalmist says that he leaned on God from before his birth. He understood how much he depended on God for life from the moment of conception. God sustained and kept him in the womb of his mother.

Listen to what God said to His people in Isaiah 46:3-4:

> *3 Listen to me, O house of Jacob, all the remnant of the house of Israel, who have been borne by me from before your birth, carried from the womb; 4 even in your old age I am he, and to gray hairs I will carry you. I have made, and I will bear; I will carry and will save.*

God made it quite clear to His people that He had borne them from before their birth. In other words, He took personal responsibility for them when they were still in their mother's womb. The one who knew them before they were conceived and formed them in the womb also watched over them from the moment they were conceived. He protected and kept them safe in the womb of their mother. The protecting work of God does not begin when we are born—even before we were brought into this world, the hand of God has been at work protecting and keeping us for the purpose He has in mind.

The Preparatory Work of God in the Womb

God calls us, forms us and protects us in the womb of our mother. God also prepares us for the work He has in mind. This preparatory work of God also begins in the womb. Consider what the apostle Paul told the Ephesians in Ephesians 2:10:

For we are his workmanship, created in Christ Jesus for good works, which God prepared beforehand that we should walk in them.

Even before we were aware of the purpose of God for our lives, He was preparing the works He had for us to accomplish. God not only prepared the circumstances in life but He also prepared us for those circumstances. The Psalmist makes this clear when he says:

15 My frame was not hidden from you, when I was being made in secret, intricately woven in the depth of the earth. 16 Your eyes saw my unformed substance; in your book were written, every one of them, the days that were formed or me, when as yet there was none of them. (Psalm 139:15-16)

While I was still in the womb of my mother being woven into the person He wanted me to be, God knew what every day in my life would bring. Every day of my life was written in His book even before I was born. He shaped me in the womb of my mother with these days in mind.

The Psalmist recognized that even before he came into this earth, he had an obligation to this wonderful Creator God. In Psalm 22:10 he says:

On you was I cast from my birth, and from my mother's womb you have been my God.

What does it mean that God is our God? It means that He is our Lord and we are submissive to Him in all things. The implication is quite clear. God is the God of the unborn. He watches over and gives them life. They in turn are under obligation to submit to Him as their Sovereign Lord.

What do we see from these passages of Scripture? God takes a very special interest in unborn children. He shapes them in the womb into the people He wants them to be. Like a great potter, He forms my life with its unique personality and appearance while it is yet in the womb of my mother. He protects unborn children and calls Himself their God. Even before I was born, God called me by name. Before I was born, God knew every day of my life and what those days would bring. He knows details about my life that still after many years of living on this earth I still do not know. I was created and shaped by God, protected by God and prepared by God for life while I was still in the womb of my mother. God's interest in me and His work in my life began in the womb and will continue even to the end of my days.

For Consideration:

Take a moment to consider the miracle of life that begins at the moment of conception. How is the creative hand of God shown in what takes place in the womb of the mother from conception?

The prophet Isaiah tells us that God bears us from the womb (Isaiah 46:3). How does God carry the unborn child in the womb? What does this tell us about the value God places on this child?

How does God prepare us for the work He has in store? How does He shape us in the womb for the calling He has placed on our lives?

Is an unborn child loved by God as much as a child born into this world? Explain.

For Prayer:

Thank the Lord for the miraculous way in which He shapes the unborn child in the womb of the mother.

Take a moment to give praise to the Lord for how He watches over the child in the womb.

Thank the Lord for the purpose He has in mind for each child conceived in the womb. Thank Him for how He shapes each one differently.

Ask the Lord to give you a sense of awe and respect for His miraculous work in the womb. Ask the Lord to forgive us as a society for not having he heart of God toward these unborn children.

5 - DESCRIPTION OF THE FRUIT OF THE WOMB

In this chapter, let's take a moment to examine a few verses that describe the unborn child in the womb of the mother. While there are many verses that describe children born into this world, my focus in this chapter is the child still in the womb.

Let's begin with Genesis 49:25. In Genesis 49, Jacob had come to the end of his life and now took the time to bless each of his children. Genesis 49:25 is part of the blessing of Jacob on his son Joseph:

25 By the God of your father who will help you, by the Almighty who will bless you with blessings from heaven above, blessings of the deep that crouches beneath, blessings of the breasts and of the womb.

Notice how Jacob told his son that the God of his fathers would bless him with many types of blessings.

Of particular significance to us is the phrase "blessings of the breasts and of the womb." Jacob makes special mention of two types of blessings in this phrase. The phrase "blessings of the breasts" is clearly a reference to the nursing child at the breast of the mother. The "blessings of the womb," however, is a reference to the unborn child being formed in the womb of the mother. For Jacob, the unborn child in the womb was as much of a blessing from God as the child nursing at his or her mother's breast. One was as valuable as the other.

Struggling with the prosperity of the wicked, the psalmist says in Psalm 17:13-14:

13 Arise, O Lord! Confront him, subdue him! Deliver my soul from the wicked by your sword, 14 from men by your hand, O Lord, from men of the world whose portion is in this life. You fill their womb with treasure; they are satisfied with children, and they leave their abundance to their infants.

The psalmist speaks very strongly against the wicked who oppressed him in this passage. "Confront him, subdue him!" he asks the Lord. These men were evil and the psalmist wanted the Lord to judge them for their evil. Having said this, however, notice how the psalmist describes the children conceived in the wombs of their women –"You fill their womb with treasure."

The "treasure" the psalmist is describing here is the unborn children of wicked men. Despite the fact that the parents of these unformed children were evil, these children were still a precious and valuable treasure. The psalmist speaks with great respect for the life of the child in the womb even though this child is the fruit of wicked parents. Every unformed child conceived in the womb is a treasure from God. A child's value does not lie in who their parents are but in the fact that they are a creation of God.

The Psalmist again speaks of the fruit of the womb in Psalm 127:3:

3 Behold, children are a heritage from the Lord, the fruit of the womb a reward.

Of particular significance is the phrase: "the fruit of the womb a reward." The child being formed in the womb of the mother is a reward from God. This child is a gift of God—an indication of His favour and blessing.

What do these three passages tell us about the unborn child? The child growing in the womb of the mother is a blessing, a treasure and a wonderful reward or gift from God. Even the unborn child of evil parents is a treasure from God. Scripture is quite clear on this matter. The fruit of the womb is to be respected. From the moment of conception this young, unformed life is to be valued and honored as a blessing of God.

For Consideration:

How does Scripture describe the fruit of the womb?

Is the value of the unformed child in the womb dependant on his or her parents?

Based on the description of the child in the womb of his or her mother, how should we see and treat the unborn child?

For Prayer:

Thank the Lord for the value He places on the unformed child in the womb.

Ask the Lord to forgive your society for not valuing unborn children as it should. Ask God to reveal the value He places on these lives.

Ask the Lord to forgive you for valuing a child based on his or her parents. Thank the Lord that each person is an individual before Him and his or her value in not dependant on the life of their parents.

6 - INFANTS WHO NEVER SEE THE LIGHT

13 Or why was I not as a hidden stillborn child, as infants who never seen the light? (Job 3:16)

The life into which a child is born is not always easy. In fact there are times when life facing that child is very cruel. In the verse quoted above, Job considered his lot in life and wished he had died in the womb. In fact, in the third chapter of his book, Job curses the day of his birth.

3 Let the day perish on which I was born, and the night that said, "A man is conceived."

Job, at this point in his life, had lost his children and all his wealth. He sat in an ash heap scratching the boils on his body wondering why he had to suffer. The agony of life was so heavy on him that he lamented the fact that God had let him be conceived and born into such a cruel world.

7 Behold, let that night be barren; let no joyful cry enter it. 8 Let those curse it who curse the day, who are ready to rouse up Leviathan. 9 Let the stars of its dawn be dark; let it hope for light, but have none, nor see the eyelids of the morning, 10 because it did not shut the doors of my mother's womb, nor hide trouble from my eyes. 11 Why did I not die at birth, come out from the womb and expire? 12 Why did the knees receive me? Or the breasts, that I should nurse? 13 For then I would have lain down and been quiet; I would have slept; then I would have been at rest. (Job 3)

Had Job never been born, he would not have agonized over the death of his children. He would not have suffered the physical affliction he was experiencing at this time. To Job, at this time, the death of a child in the womb was a blessing because it spared him or her from the terror and pain of life.

He expressed these feelings further in Job 10:18-19 when he said:

18 Why did you bring me out from the womb? Would that I had died before any eye had seen me 19 and were as though I had not been, carried from the womb to the grave.

Job was not alone in these thoughts. In Jeremiah 20, we read how the prophet was beaten and put in stocks to be publicly humiliated. Struggling with what had happened to him for preaching the word of God, the prophet prayed:

7 O Lord, you have deceived me, and I was deceived; you are stronger than I, and you have prevailed. I have become a laughingstock all the day; everyone mocks me 8 For whenever I speak, I cry out, I shout, "Violence and destruction!" For the word of God has become for me a reproach and derision all day long.

Here was a man who struggled with the fact that he preached what God had given him to preach and yet experienced such rejection and mocking. As he cried out to God about his bitter lot in life, Jeremiah declares:

14 Cursed be the day on which I was born! The day when my mother bore me, let it not be blessed! 15 Cursed be the man who brought the news to my father, "A son is born to you," making him glad. 16 Let that man be like the cities that the Lord overthrew without pity; let him hear a cry in the morning and an alarm at noon, 17 because He did not kill me in the womb; so my mother would have been my grave, and her womb forever great. 18 Why did I come out from the womb to see toil and sorrow, and spend my days in shame? (Jeremiah 20)

Jeremiah literally cursed the man who brought news of his birth because he did not abort him in the womb (see Jeremiah 20:17).

Here before us we see deep grief in these servants of God. Their grief was so intense that they wished they had died in the womb, never to see the light of day. The pain they experienced in life was more than they felt they could bear. They cried out questioning why they were conceived or aborted before they saw such suffering.

Listen to the words of Solomon in Ecclesiastes 6:3:

> *3 If a man fathers a hundred children and lives many years, so that the days of his years are many but his soul is not satisfied with life's good things, and he also has no burial, I say that a stillborn child is better off than he.*

Solomon speaks here about a man who is richly blessed. The sign of this great blessing is his many children and long years of life. This man, however, is not satisfied in his soul. His life has no meaning for him. Solomon tells us that this man, though richly blessed, lived a cursed life without satisfaction in the many blessings he has been given. He went as far as to say that it would have been better for him to have been a stillborn child than to go through life depressed and unsatisfied.

Job, Jeremiah and Solomon seem to be saying that there are situations where it would be better to die in the womb or be aborted than to be born. It is important that we examine what these men are saying in the context of God's purpose for the life of the unborn child. There are several points we need to make about these comments of Job, Solomon and Jeremiah.

First, the comments of Job, Jeremiah and Solomon must be seen in their context. They are the expressions of human hearts unsure as to how to handle the purpose of God. Job and Jeremiah are in the midst of a great trial of faith. They are open and honest with God and speak plainly what is on their mind. At this point, they wished they had never been born. The pain they experienced in life made them wish they had died in their mother's womb. They are *not* teaching us that to kill children in the womb is to do him or her a favour by sparing them the troubles of life. They are simply expressing their feelings in a moment of pain.

Secondly, we must also consider how God responded to Job and Jeremiah after they declared that they wished they had died in the womb. He listened carefully to their cry and responded. To Job, God said:

> *1 Then the Lord answered Job out of the whirlwind and said: 2 "Who is this that darkens counsel by words without knowledge?"*

In other words, God was asking Job if he really knew what he was talking about. He spoke words without knowledge.

To Jeremiah the Lord said:

5 If you have raced with men on foot, and they have wearied you, how will you compete with horses? And if in a safe land you are so trusting, what will you do in the thicket of the Jordan?

God reminded Jeremiah that He had an even greater plan for his life. He was going to take him to the "thicket of the Jordan" but first he needed to learn to compete with horses. These problems he complained about now were designed to train him for an even greater work. God shows these men that there was purpose in the pain they struggled so deeply with. Complaining and wishing they had been aborted in the womb only showed that they did not know the mind of God nor did they trust His purpose.

Suffering and pain are normal parts of life in a sinful world. The Lord Jesus had to face Satan head on. He was rejected throughout His life. At his birth, Herod tried to kill Him. As he ministered, people took advantage of Him. He would die a cruel death at the age of thirty. He took on the sin of the world. He saw the Father turn His face from Him as He bore our sins. Would it have been better that He had never been born? Certainly not! The work He accomplished in those few short years brought salvation and forgiveness to God's people.

The apostle Paul lived a life of struggle and pain. He was beaten and stoned for the message he preached. At times, he was left for dead after being stoned. He experienced more rejection and suffering in life than many of us will ever experience. Would it have been better for him never to have been born? Certainly not! The message he preached changed countless lives. His writing continues to bring many into the kingdom.

Surely we need to understand that these men needed to be brought onto this earth and suffer so that we could know the salvation of God. None of us enjoy pain and suffering but often the purpose of God is accomplished in it. Job, Jeremiah, Jesus and Paul were all mightily used of God through the things they suffered to accomplish His purpose.

Would things have been easier for them had they never been born? From a human perspective, they would not have had to face the suffering they endured. But from a divine perspective, the purpose of God would not have been accomplished. The suffering of these men brought life and hope to many. What they endured brings us great blessing. I for one am thankful for their lives.

Yes, Job and Jeremiah struggled with their lot in life wishing they had never been born. God, however, used them to push back the darkness of evil. I am thankful that they were born and proved faithful to that purpose despite the pain they endured.

For Consideration:

Have you ever been in a situation that you felt you could not bear? What was your response in that time? How did the Lord take you through it?

What do we learn from this chapter about struggle and difficulties in life? Will all children be born to a life of ease and comfort?

Take a moment to consider the struggles of Job, Jeremiah, Paul and Jesus? Are you glad they were born and endured this suffering? What was the result of their faithfulness?

Is it really better for a child not to be born to a life of suffering? How does God use suffering to accomplish His purpose?

For Prayer:

Thank the Lord that even though we may be born to suffer, He is able to use this to accomplish great good.

Thank the Lord for the privilege of being born into this world and called to be an instrument of change.

Ask the Lord to give you grace to be faithful to what the Lord has called you to do, despite the pain and struggle that is involved.

7 - SUMMARY AND CONCLUSION

Over the course of the last six chapters, we have sought to understand the teaching of Scripture concerning life in the womb. In this final chapter, I would like to summarize what we have seen.

Our God is an all-knowing and eternal God. He knew us even before we were conceived and had a purpose for our lives (Genesis 17:19). He knew all the details of our life and how our lives would unfold (Luke 1:13-14).

In the wombs of our mothers, He called us by name (Isaiah 49:1). He knew us personally and took special interest in us. While we were still being shaped in the womb, God called us and set us apart for His special purpose (Jeremiah 1:5). He shaped our bodies and personalities in the womb to suit us for the call He had placed on our lives.

God creates, knits us together (Psalm 139:13-14) and protects us in the womb of our mothers (Isaiah 46:3-4). There in the womb, He prepares us for our responsibilities in life (Psalm 139:15-16).

There is evidence in Scripture that the Lord also does a spiritual work in the life of the unborn child. John the Baptist was filled with the Holy Spirit in the womb (Luke 1:15). Jacob and Esau fought in the womb of their mother (Genesis 25:22), the beginning of a great spiritual battle that would take place for generations to come.

Scripture describes the fruit of the womb as a blessing (Genesis 49:25), a treasure (Psalm 17:13-14) and a reward (Psalm 127:3). This shows us the value God places on the unformed substance of these children yet to be born.

It is true that these children will be born into a sinful world filled with grief and struggle. That suffering and grief, however, is not without purpose. Those who come to Him have the privilege of knowing their Creator and fellowshipping with Him in even the worst trials. They are His instruments to accomplish His purpose on this earth. They have the privilege of walking in His power and authority and the joy of knowing that when their task on earth is completed, they will enter His presence for all eternity separated from sin and its effects.

What does this study show us about the value of the unborn child? It shows us that each child is the work of the Heavenly Father. It shows us that God has a purpose for the unformed child. He values each life and knows each one by name.

It would seem to me that we are called to respect

the life God is forming and protecting in the womb. This is a creation of God and one for which He has a purpose. Does every child born walk in that purpose of God? I'm afraid many do not. We have all fallen short of the standard of God. Some will reject their Creator completely. Others will violently oppose the purpose of God and become instruments of Satan. Those who receive Him, however, become His instruments to advance His kingdom.

It would be wonderful to think that every child would be born to a loving father and mother. In this world of sin and evil, however, this is not always the case. There are women who have experienced the horrors of rape and sexual violence. The children born to these mothers, however, are still precious in God's eyes. Many will see evils they should never have to see. Some will face struggles in life no child should ever have to face. Despite this, however, they are to be valued as the creation of God. If anything, this is a call for the people of God to stand up and be the parents, counsellors, encouragers and supporters that these children need.

I have purposely not spoken about the matter of abortion in this study. What we have examined, however, should help us to see the incredible value God places on life in the womb. As I have worked through the various passages of Scripture related to life before birth, I have been struck by the fact that my God knew me, called me and valued me long before I was born. I was loved and cared for in the womb. I praise God who took this much interest in me. I want to live my life to accomplish the purpose for which I was conceived. I am renewed in my understanding of the value He places on every child in the womb, no matter the circumstance of their conception. May the Lord be pleased to use this study to enable each reader to stand with God in valuing and caring for the fruit of every womb for His glory and praise.

For Consideration:

What does this study teach us about the value of the unformed child in the womb of the mother?

According to what we have seen in this study, what should be our attitude toward the child in the womb?

When does life begin? If the child in the womb is considered to be a person from the time of conception, how does the law and requirements of God for the treatment of all people apply to the unborn child?

For Prayer:

Take a moment to thank the Lord that He knew you before you were conceived.

Thank the Lord for how He formed you and valued you in the womb of your mother.

Ask the Lord to help you to see each child as a creation of God. Ask God to help you to value life whether it be in the womb or born into this world.

Thank the Lord that although we are born into a sinful world, we can know His presence and power to accomplish His purpose. Thank Him for that privilege of knowing Him and being forgiven of your sins.

Take a moment to pray for those who do not yet know Him as their Saviour and Lord. Ask God to reveal Himself to them in a way that gives them hope and purpose in life.

ABOUT THE AUTHOR

Light To My Path Book Distribution

Light To My Path (LTMP) is a book writing and distribution ministry reaching out to needy Christian workers in Asia, Latin America, and Africa. Many Christian workers in developing countries do not have the resources necessary to obtain Bible training or purchase Bible study materials for their ministries and personal encouragement.

F. Wayne Mac Leod is a member of Action International Ministries and has been writing these books with a goal to distribute them to needy pastors and Christian workers around the world. To date thousands of books are being used in preaching, teaching, evangelism and encouragement of local believers in over sixty countries. Books have now been translated a number of languages. The goal is to make them available to as many believers as possible.

The ministry of LTMP is a faith based ministry and we trust the Lord for the resources necessary to distribute the books for the encouragement and strengthening of believers around the world. Would you pray that the Lord would open doors for the translation and further distribution of these books?

For more information about Light To My Path Book Distribution visit our website at www.lighttomypath.ca